# More Floopydoos

## by Refried Bean

# More Floopydoos

## by Refried Bean

Thank you to all my
family, friends, teachers,
and everyone else
who has helped me.


this book is dedicated to
Eggy, Strawberry, and
all the precious sweetingest punkin pies

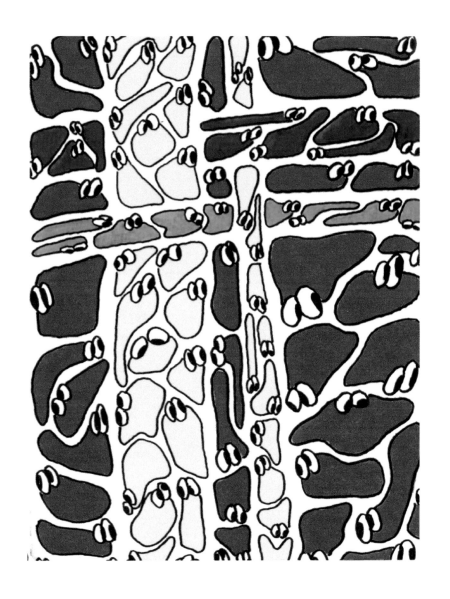

# Patternerbles
## by Refried Bean

# Patternerbles

## by Refried Bean

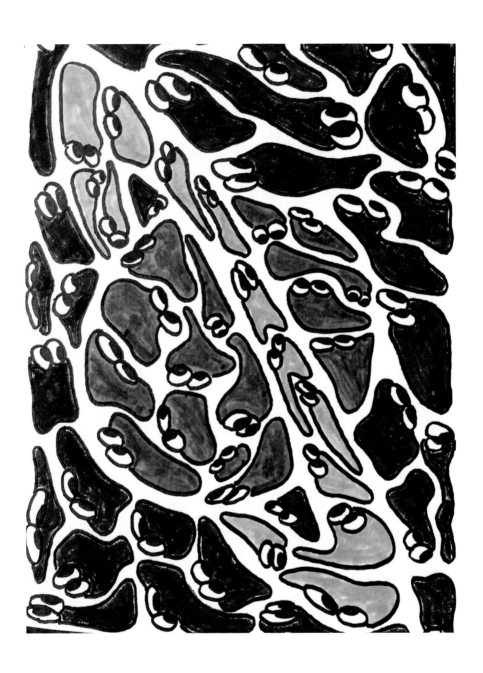

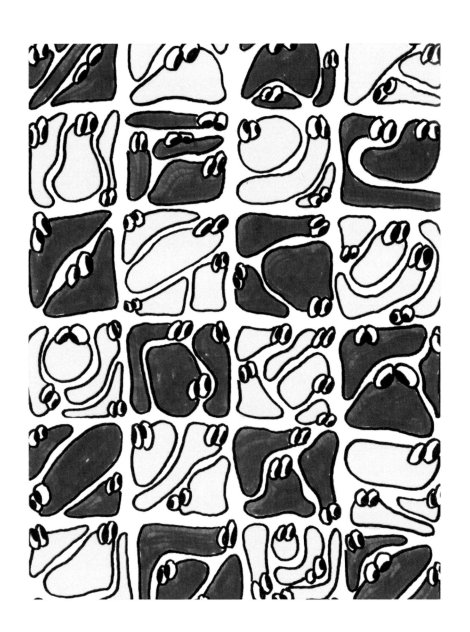

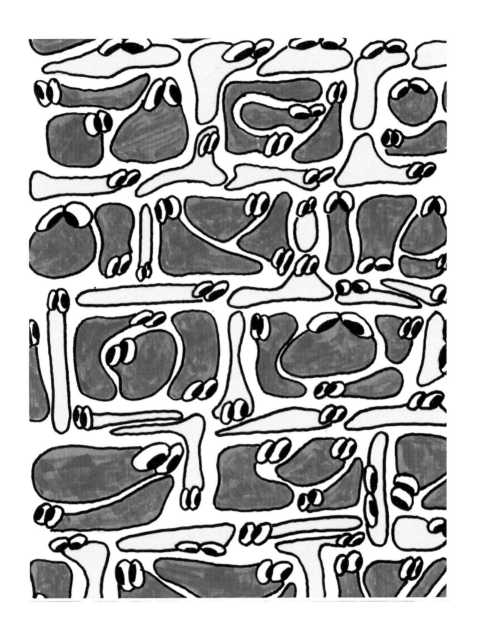

# Also by Refried Bean:
## *Floopydoos and Floofs with Lines*

Refried Bean is from Greenville, SC.
Refried worked in a bookstore for twelve years
and has an M.F.A. in Writing
from Vermont College of Fine Arts.
Refried has three pet guinea pigs named
Fred, Roger, and Dave.

Made in United States
North Haven, CT
24 May 2022

19486740R00042